125 MORE

Learn to Read

Activities

Fun Lessons to Teach Your Child to Read

RAE PRITCHETT, MEd, CAGS

callisto publishing
an imprint of Sourcebooks

Copyright © 2024 by Callisto Publishing LLC

Cover and internal design © by Callisto Publishing LLC

Illustrations © Robin Boyer with the following exceptions:

© N.Savranska/Shutterstock: cover (owl); © funkyplayerL/Shutterstock: throughout (chevron pattern); © Joel and Ashley Selby: 3 (queen), 12 (mad emoji, pen), 12, 28, 29 (bell), 14 (puppy), 23 (scissors), 23, 50 (thermometer), 25, 130 (sad emoji), 26 (hat), 28 (pin), 30 (runner), 32 (pine tree), 33 (cape), 36 (kite), 41, 87 (clapping hands), 46 (piggy bank), 50 (kitchen), 52, 68 (happy emoji), 61 (hand soap, pool), 71. 112 (baseball), 83 (slides & ladders), 87 (mouth), 102 (cup), 107 (leg, stick); © Collaborate: 19 (log); © ayelet-keshet/Shutterstock: 70 (friends); © Rhianna Marie Chan: 130 (laptop)

Series Designer: Will Mack and Michael Cook

Art Director: Jennifer Hsu

Art Producer: Sue Bischofberger

Editor: Laura Apperson

Production Editor: Jael Fogle

Production Manager: Martin Worthington

Published by Callisto Publishing LLC C/O Sourcebooks LLC

P.O. Box 4410, Naperville, Illinois 60567-4410

(630) 961-3900

callistopublishing.com

This product conforms to all applicable CPSC and CPSIA standards.

Source of Production: 1010 Printing Asia Limited, Kwun Tong, Hong Kong, China

Date of Production: December 2023

Run Number: 5035977

Printed and bound in China.

OGP 10 9 8 7 6 5 4 3 2 1

CONTENTS

INTRODUCTION

Hi! My name is Rae Pritchett. Welcome to *125 More Learn to Read Activities*. As an educator for over 20 years, my passion for teaching students is grounded in the belief that reading is one of the most important skills you can foster in a child. The ability to read affects a child's entire academic experience as well as their overall success in life. I became a teacher to give students the power to achieve their fullest potential and beyond, and I wrote this book to help you also be that teacher!

Inside this book are 125 on-the-page activities to help teach beginning readers (ages 5 to 7) the skills they need to learn to read. As they work through the exercises, your child will expand their letter/sound knowledge, which will allow them to read words with complex letter-sound relationships and multiple syllables.

125 More Learn to Read Activities is a companion book to *Learn to Read Activity Book*, which focused on single letter sounds and short vowel one-syllable words like /cat/. If your child already has these skills, then this book is a great match for your child's reading needs!

We have learned a great deal about how children learn to read in the last few decades. This research has helped us improve the way we teach our children how to read. The activities in this book are rooted in that research and are designed to build your child's reading confidence and help set them up to become successful readers. When your child has completed all the activities in this book, I hope they will be comfortable reading more complex words and will develop a love of reading.

FOR PARENTS, CAREGIVERS, AND TEACHERS

How to Use This Book

This book expands upon a child's knowledge of the phonics skills and sight words introduced in the *Learn to Read Activity Book*. If your child hasn't finished *Learn to Read Activity Book*, review it with them and gauge their skill level. They may be ready for this, or they may not. That's okay! We just want to avoid frustrating them (and you) by jumping too far ahead. It features 125 on-the-page activities divided into eight sections, each focusing on a core skill:

1. Word Sounds

2. Vowel Sounds (and Y)

3. Blends

4. Digraphs

5. Sight Words

6. Syllables

7. Compound Words

8. Prefix and Suffix (Inflectional Endings only)

Some sections begin with one or two review skill pages and practice skills introduced in the *Learn to Read Activity Book*. The activities in each section increase in difficulty, building upon the review skills and introducing new skills. This progression of difficulty builds confidence.

Before you dive in, here are some tips for helping your child get the most out of this book:

- **Preview a section yourself before your child begins.** Familiarizing yourself with the content will help you prepare for the activities your child will encounter, understand the purpose of the section, and activate your own knowledge about the skill. Take this one step further by completing the activities yourself so you can learn the book's approach to developing each skill.

- **Read the section introduction.** Each section starts with a brief introduction that explains the specific breakdown of that section's skill. This information is important because it will define the skill for you, explain the goal of the section, and explain the best way to support learning the skill. Tips for working through the skill will be included!
- **Work through the book in chronological order.** Have the child begin with section one and work through each section from the beginning to the end.
- **Ask children to go back and repeat activities.** This is called spiral review, and it is important for learning. These repeated practice opportunities build automaticity of reading skills. Automaticity, or fast, accurate, and effortless word identification, is essential to proficient reading.
- **Include other reading experiences.** Introduce children to read-alouds, book discussions, reading practice with decodable readers, and hands-on reading and spelling activities—such as reading words that the child has written in a tray of salt or made out of play dough.

Most importantly, be patient with your beginning reader. Learning to read is difficult, so let the child guide the pace of learning by observing their emotional cues.

Notice:

- Is the child having fun?
- Does the child appear frustrated?
- Is the child starting to feel defeated and giving up?

We all need breaks! Recognize when your child needs one. You can read more about this in the Motivating Your Child section (page ix).

The goal of learning to read is not only about reading comprehension, but also about developing a love of reading. Because of this, it's important that we do not push children to frustration when they are learning to read. Instead, make learning to read challenging *and* fun!

How to Set Your Child Up for Success

All children learn differently. Let your child learn at their own pace. It's also important to have realistic goals for your child. Children ages 5 to 7 are working to be able to:

1. Delete syllables in words (i.e., "Say /cupcake/. Now say /cupcake/, but don't say /cake/.")

2. Delete phonemes (units of sound created by letters or letter combinations) in words to form new words (i.e., delete /t/ sound in /went/ to get /when/)

3. Substitute phonemes in words (i.e., say /keep/, but instead of /k/ say /s/)

The goal is to be successful readers and spellers of closed syllable words like /cat/ and /swam/.

Motivating Your Child

How can you keep your child motivated to read? Try these tips!

Teaching Growth Mindset

A child with a growth mindset believes they can succeed with hard work. Build this mindset by praising your child for their efforts.

Empower your child with growth mindset phrases like . . .
- "I'll try a new strategy," instead of "I give up."
- "This may take some effort," instead of "This is too hard."

Verbal Praise

Verbal praise is very motivating! Give your child praise to build a positive self-image. Here are some examples:
- "Wow! You spelled a difficult word."
- "Great job!"
- "You are really working hard, and your reading shows that!"

Praise helps your child recognize their successes and feel proud. This boosts performance!

Offer Choice

Offering choices gives a child control. This is motivational, helps to grow a child's confidence, and teaches responsibility. Here are some examples:

- "I see you're tired. Would you like me to circle the ones you tell me to?"
- "Do you want to read the sight words while marching?"

Rewards

Connecting a reward to self-competence motivates children's efforts and increases perseverance. Do this by matching the reward to the effort needed for the activity.

Each section starts with review activities, so these rewards can be small, like stickers. Increase rewards to things like trips to the park or extra playtime when activities get harder.

More Tips and Tricks

Readers are made, not born, so here are some tips and tricks to help your child's reading grow:

1. Say words slowly and stretch out sounds.

2. Tap out the phonemes, or sounds, in words. Tap on the table or down your arm while saying a word, one tap per sound (t-r-i-p, c-a-t). Run your hand back over the sounds from the beginning, and blend the sounds to say the word.

3. Clap out syllables in words.

4. Write words from this book on index cards so your child can practice reading them. Ask your child to come up with rhyming words for those words. Write the rhyming words on the back of the cards to practice the spelling pattern (/rat/ rhymes with /cat/, the spelling pattern is /at/).

5. Get multisensory with your teaching! Have your child read words from this book (or from the cards you made from Tip 4), and then make them out of play dough. Try writing them with a fingertip on a cookie sheet lined with a thin layer of table salt.

6. Have your child read familiar books again and again.

7. Read aloud to your child, and talk about what you read.

Skill 1: Word Sounds

In this section, children will use their knowledge of word sounds to read and spell VC (vowel-consonant) and CVC (consonant-vowel-consonant) words.

VC words contain a vowel followed by a consonant, like in /at/ or /on/. CVC words contain a vowel closed in by a consonant on either side, like in /cat/ or /pin/.

Practicing letter patterns and their sounds will help your child recognize them automatically in words. For example, show your child that if you change the /c/ to /s/ in the word /cat/, you get /sat/. Once a child learns the letter pattern /at/, the child can read a ton of words in the /at/ word family!

Here are three tips to help you help your child learn word sounds:

1. Practice letter sounds. Show a letter (/o/) or letter pattern (/am/). Have your child say the letter and its sound aloud.
2. Phonetic awareness is required to read! Say words aloud and then ask, "What sound do you hear at the beginning, middle, and/or end of the word?"
3. Continue phonetic awareness. Place an object on the table, like a block, for each sound in a word. Touch each block, and say its sound. Blend the sounds to say the word.

Let's Review A to M

SKILL: CONSONANTS A TO M

Trace each letter with your finger and say its name. Repeat the letter's sound five times. Then say its keyword and color the picture.

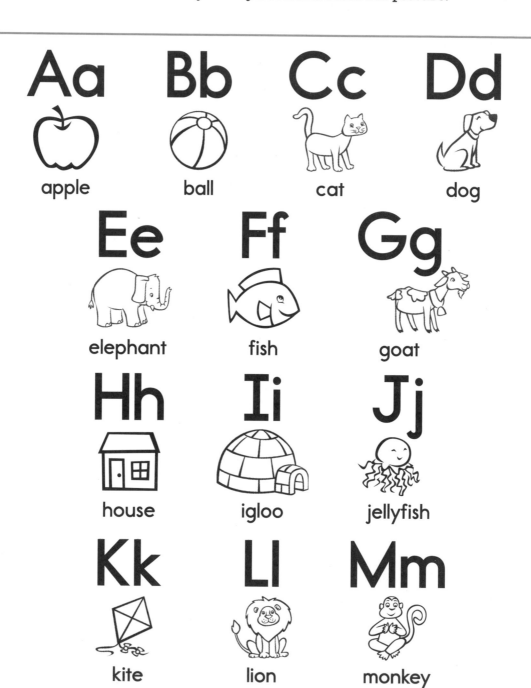

Aa — apple

Bb — ball

Cc — cat

Dd — dog

Ee — elephant

Ff — fish

Gg — goat

Hh — house

Ii — igloo

Jj — jellyfish

Kk — kite

Ll — lion

Mm — monkey

Let's Review N to Z

SKILL: CONSONANTS N TO Z

Trace each letter with your finger and say its name. Repeat the letter's sound five times. Then say its keyword and color the picture.

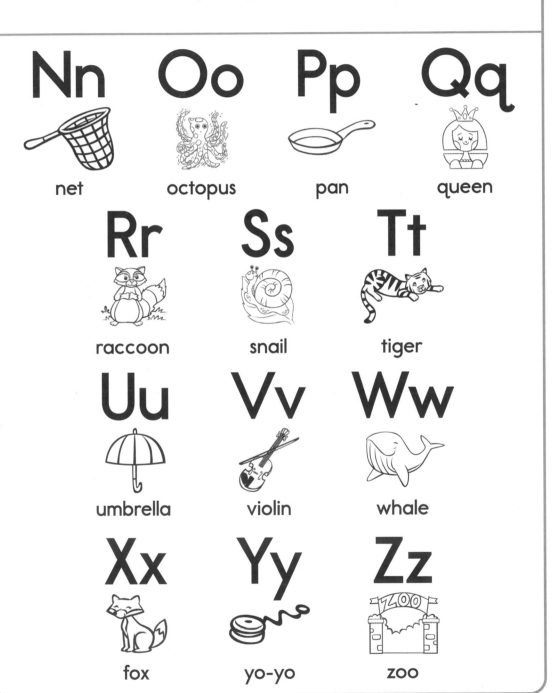

Nn — net

Oo — octopus

Pp — pan

Qq — queen

Rr — raccoon

Ss — snail

Tt — tiger

Uu — umbrella

Vv — violin

Ww — whale

Xx — fox

Yy — yo-yo

Zz — zoo

Blend and Match

SKILL: BLENDING WORD SOUNDS

Touch the dots and say each sound in each word. Then slide your finger through the sounds to blend them into a word. Draw a line to connect each word to the matching picture.

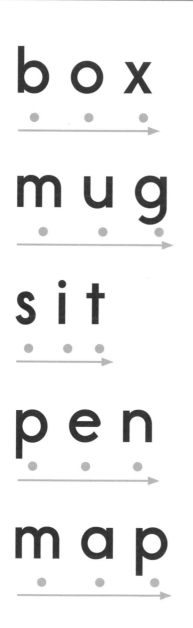

Blending and Circling

SKILL: BLENDING WORD SOUNDS

Touch the dots and say each sound in each word. Then slide your finger through the sounds to blend them into a word. Circle the picture that matches the word.

Rhyme Time

SKILL: RHYMING WORDS

Help Kim and Tim get to the pool by following the words that rhyme with *bog* through the maze.

125 More Learn to Read Activities

Circle First

SKILL: IDENTIFYING BEGINNING SOUNDS

Say the word for each picture. Circle the letter that you hear at the *beginning* of each word.

c r t	g j p	r m l
e b p	g s j	c x r
v n w	c z m	g t w

Circle Last

SKILL: IDENTIFYING ENDING SOUNDS

Say the word for each picture. Circle the letter that you hear at the *end* of each word.

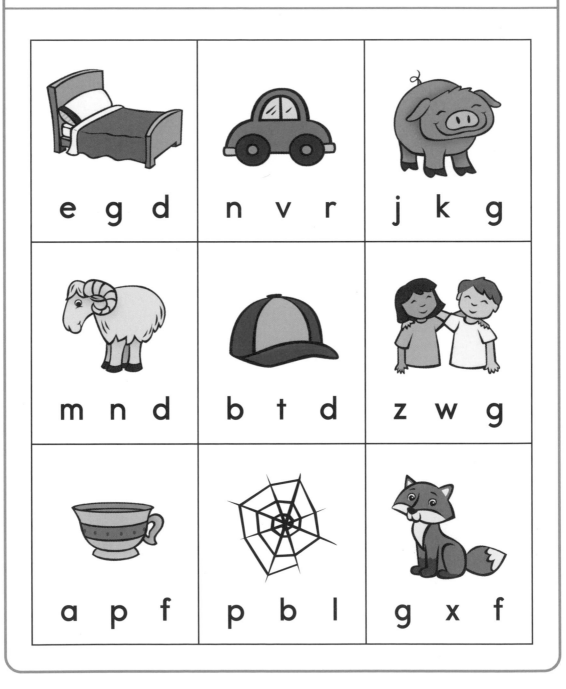

e g d	n v r	j k g
m n d	b t d	z w g
a p f	p b l	g x f

Beginning Match

SKILL: IDENTIFYING BEGINNING SOUNDS

Say the word for each picture. Draw a line to the letter you hear at the *beginning* of the word.

c

l

s

b

j

Ending Match

SKILL: IDENTIFYING ENDING SOUNDS

Say the word for each picture. Draw a line to the letter you hear at the *end* of the word.

p

k

r

g

sh

Find That Shopper

SKILL: SORTING WORD FAMILIES

Kat, Sam, Dan, and Jack went shopping. They each only bought items that rhyme with their names. Can you figure out what each child bought? Write each item under the name that it rhymes with.

Who bought a ...

ram   mat
fan   snack
pack   pan
cat   yam
ham

Kat	Sam

Dan	Jack

Who bought the most items?

Color the Sounds

SKILL: IDENTIFYING SOUNDS

Follow the directions for each set of boxes.

Color the boxes that have words that begin with the letter V

Color the boxes that have words that begin with the letter B

Color the boxes that have words that end with the letter D

Color the boxes that have words that end with the letter P

First Sounds

SKILL: IDENTIFYING BEGINNING SOUNDS

Write in the letter of the missing first sound.

_____ ell

_____ eaf

_____ all

_____ ow

_____ ap

_____ arm

_____ og

_____ aw

_____ ar

Last Sounds

SKILL: IDENTIFYING ENDING SOUNDS

Write in the letter of the missing last sound.

bo____

cu____

ho____

wi____

bu____

be____

ra____

slee____

ra____

Shopping for Sounds

SKILL: IDENTIFYING BEGINNING AND ENDING SOUNDS

Today you are going shopping for sounds. Circle the correct letter you need to buy to finish each word.

	ow ___	p j l
	___ at	p d b
	___ ips	k l d
	ca ___	g t e

What letters do you have in your shopping cart?

_____

Sentence Match

SKILL: WORD SOUNDS IN SENTENCES

Read each sentence. Draw a line to match the sentence to the picture.

We have a cat.
●   ●   ●   ●

I am at bat.
●   ●   ●   ●

I have a mop.
●   ●   ●   ●

We sit.
●   ●

Spell It!

SKILL: SPELLING WORDS

Spell each word by putting one letter in each of the boxes next to it.

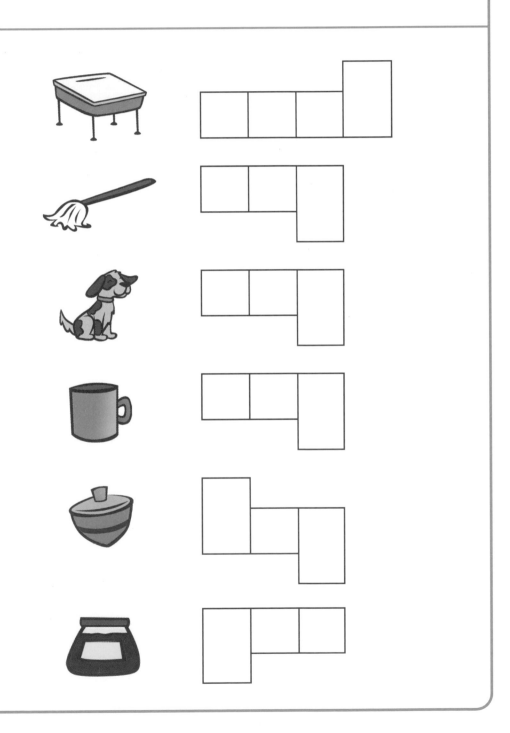

Word Detective

SKILL: MANIPULATING WORD SOUNDS

Read each clue and write the answer on the line.

We have a 🐱 . _____

Change the first letter in the word 🐱 and you

get 🦇 . _____

Change the /t/ sound in the word for 🦇 to a

/g/ sound. What word do you get? _____

Change the /a/ sound in the word for 🛍 to a /i/

sound. What word do you get? _____

Change the first letter in your last word, and you will

know that I am a 🐷 . _____

Complete the Sentences

SKILL: READING WITH WORD SOUNDS

Read each sentence and circle the word that best fits the sentence.

The boy was sat / sad.

The mug is hot / hit.

We put a log / lop on the fire.

I fit / fill the cup with milk.

The kid hit the bell / ball with a bat / bot.

Write a Story

SKILL: READING WITH WORD SOUNDS

Read the words in the word bank. Then read the story. Choose a word from the word bank to write on each line to complete the story.

cat, rat, dog, bush

A cat sat in a _____ .

A _____ had a baseball.

The cat saw a _____ .

The dog saw the _____ .

The _____ ran to the cat.

The cat chased the _____ .

Skill 2: Vowel (and Y) Sounds

In this section, your child will learn the vowels—A, E, I, O, U—and the sounds they make, including short vowels, long vowels, and the common long vowel teams of /ai/, /ay/, /ea/, /ee/, /oa/, and /oe/.

Short vowels sounds are made without closing your mouth or teeth. Long vowels "say their names" like the A in the word cake, or they say the name of the first letter in the vowel team like the /ai/ in train.

Your child will also learn that Y can sometimes be a vowel and that it can make the long /i/ sound in words like "spy" and the long /e/ sound in words like "happy."

These tips can help you support your child in learning vowel (and Y) sounds:

1. Listen for short vowels. Say a word. Then draw a line for each sound you hear. Touch each line while saying each sound, and write its corresponding letter on the line.
2. Make a string of rhyming words. These are called word families. They make learning short vowels easier.
3. Learn long vowels by listening for the vowel sounds in long vowel words versus short vowel words. Say to your child, "Say cake." Ask your child, "Do you hear a long vowel or short vowel sound?"

Vowel Sound Circle

SKILL: IDENTIFYING MIDDLE VOWEL SOUNDS

Every word below has a vowel! Say the word for each picture. Circle the vowel sound that you hear in the middle.

a e i o u

a e i o u

a e i o u

a e i o u

a e i o u

Vowel Play

SKILL: SPELLING WORDS WITH VOWEL SOUNDS

Read each clue on the left side. Follow the directions and write the new word on the lines to the right—one letter on each line. Read the word you wrote.

Spell the word.	___ ___ ___
Read the word you wrote above. Change the A to an O.	___ ___ ___
Read the word you wrote above. Change the H to a C.	___ ___ ___
Read the word you wrote above. Change O to a U.	___ ___ ___

Colorful Caterpillar

SKILL: IDENTIFYING SHORT VOWEL SOUNDS

Read the words in the caterpillar and color it by following these directions:

Color the spaces blue that have words with the /a/ sound.

Color the spaces yellow that have words with the /e/ sound.

Color the spaces green that have words with the /i/ sound.

Color the spaces red that have words with the /o/ sound.

Color the spaces purple that have words with the /u/ sound.

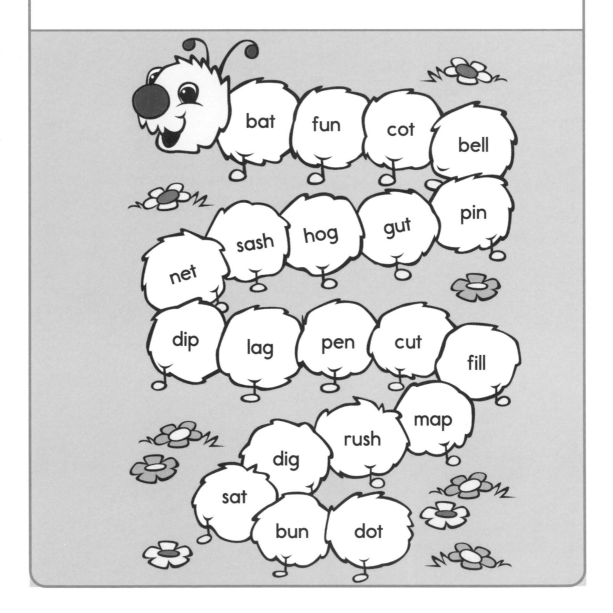

Baby Fly!

SKILL: Y AS A VOWEL SOUND

The letter Y can sometimes be a vowel, but it has two different sounds. At the end of one-syllable words, Y often has the long /i/ sound . When the Y is at the end of a two-syllable word, it often has a long /e/ sound.

Say the word for each picture and listen for the vowel sound. Draw a line to the /e/ or /i/ sound that matches the sound you hear in the word.

Vowel Shopping

SKILL: IDENTIFYING SHORT VOWEL SOUNDS

Arun has to shop for vowels at the mall. Help Arun organize his list by vowel sounds so he can shop faster. Read each word in the list. Notice the vowel sound you hear. Write the word under the correct column.

List:

sock   mitt   map

net   nut   hat

Short /a/ Words	Short /e/ Words	Short /i/ Words

Short /o/ Words	Short /u/ Words

Feather Fun

SKILL: IDENTIFYING SHORT VOWEL SOUNDS

Read the words in the peacock and color it by following these directions.

Color the spaces blue that have words with the /a/ sound.
Color the spaces yellow that have words with the /e/ sound.
Color the spaces green that have words with the /i/ sound.
Color the spaces purple that have words with the /u/ sound.

Vowel Roundup

SKILL: IDENTIFYING SHORT VOWEL SOUNDS

The vowels have gotten loose. Time to round them up! Warm up by touching each dot in each word while saying its sound. Then slide through the sounds to blend them into a word. Draw a line to the matching picture.

Now, it's time to round up the vowels! Circle the vowel in each word.

Rhyme Time

SKILL: RHYMING SHORT VOWEL SOUNDS

Fill in the missing vowel (A, E, I, O, or U) to make a word that rhymes with each picture.

	rhymes with . . .	sh ____ ll
	rhymes with . . .	b ____ x
	rhymes with . . .	m ____ p
	rhymes with . . .	b ____ n
	rhymes with . . .	c ____ t
	rhymes with . . .	t ____ p

Run, Bud, Run!

SKILL: READ WORDS WITH SHORT VOWEL SOUNDS

Bud loves to run! Help Bud run through the maze by following all the words that have the /u/ sound.

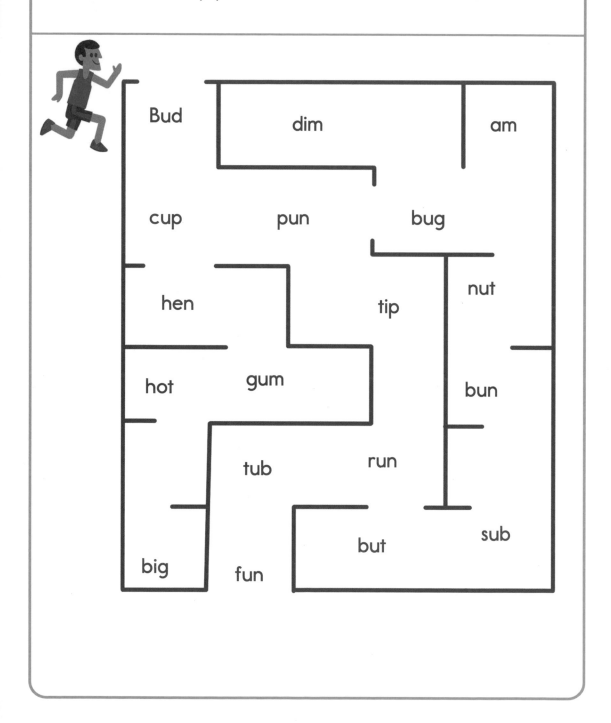

Bud

dim

am

cup

pun

bug

hen

nut

tip

hot

gum

bun

tub

run

big

fun

but

sub

The Train's Trip

SKILL: SPELLING WITH SHORT VOWEL SOUNDS

The train is carrying words to children who need them, but it has been a bumpy trip! Help by filling in the missing vowels (A, E, I, O, or U) that it lost on the bumps! Write each missing vowel in the pink train car for each word.

Bossy E

SKILL: IDENTIFYING LONG VOWEL SOUNDS

When the letter E comes at the end of a word after a vowel and a single consonant, the E makes the vowel "say its name," like the O in the word "robe."

Read each short vowel word. Draw a line to its long vowel match.

Short Vowel Words   Long Vowel Words

can

tube

pin

robe

Rob

cane

tub

pine

Say the Vowel Name

SKILL: READING LONG VOWEL SOUNDS

Add a bossy E to each word to spell it correctly. Then read the word.

cap ____	not ____	kit ____	con ____
bik ____	cub ____	cak ____	mul ____

Vowel Teams

SKILL: IDENTIFYING VOWEL TEAM SOUNDS

When vowels team up, they say the name of the first vowel in the pair. For example:

The /ai/ in train says the name of the letter A.

Say the word for each picture. Match the picture to the vowel name you hear in the word.

Long and Short of It

SKILL: READING LONG AND SHORT VOWEL SOUNDS

Nat and Nate made a mess. Help Nat and Nate sort the long and short vowel sounds into bags! Read each word. Write the word in the bag that is labeled with that word's vowel sound. Cross out the word in the list after you write it.

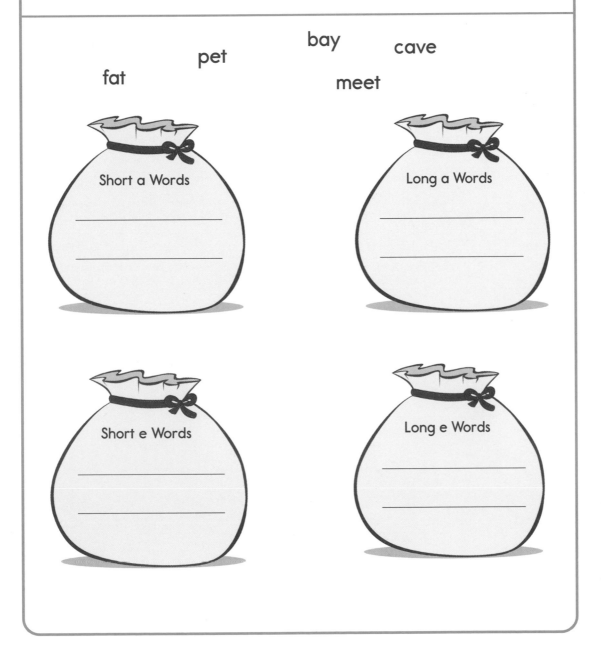

fat

pet

bay

cave

meet

Short a Words

Long a Words

Short e Words

Long e Words

Sentence Circle

SKILL: READING WORDS WITH LONG VOWEL SOUNDS

Read each sentence and circle the word that fits best.

I flew a kit / kite.

I ran home / hole.

He is a cub / cube.

Mom put on a rob / robe.

Skill 3: Blends

The goal of this section is for your child to be able to read two-letter consonant blends at the beginning and end of single and double closed-syllable words. A consonant blend is when two combined consonants make their own sound. Blends can be at the beginning of words, like /st/ in /stop/, and at the ends of words, like /-mp/ in /lamp/.

The activities in this section will teach your child that consonant blends are chunks that they will learn to recognize in words. By teaching your child to apply their knowledge of letter blends to a variety of combinations, they should be able to read words containing different blends without memorizing each blend's sound.

Here are three tips to help you help your child learn blends:

1. Phonological awareness increases children's reading skills! Say words with blends aloud (i.e., trap, sink). Ask the child where they hear the blend in the word.
2. Practice multisensory blending! Touch each letter, say its sound, and then go back and say the sounds faster, to blend sounds together quickly.
3. Make a math connection to teach blends! Write blends like math equations to teach your child to read blends in a word: $b + l = bl$

Star Blends

SKILL: IDENTIFYING WORDS WITH BEGINNING BLENDS

Let's review the blends we learned in the *Learn to Read Activity Book*!

They are: /bl-/, /cl-/, /fl-/, /gl-/, /br-/, /cr-/, /dr-/, /fr-/, /gr-/, /pr-/, /tr-/, /sm-/, /sc-/, and /st-/.

Read the word in each star. Color the star if the word has a blend.

Follow the Blends

SKILL: IDENTIFYING WORDS WITH BEGINNING BLENDS

Follow the words with blends to help Dara get to Ali on the farm.

START   flap   grab   stake

grip

small

frog

blot

sip

club

fit

flag

dig

stay

jot

FINISH

drip

Beginning Blends Match-Up

SKILL: SPELLING WORDS WITH BEGINNING BLENDS

Read the list of beginning blends. Then read the word endings. Draw a line to match each beginning blend with a word ending to make a real word. Write each word on the line next to the picture that matches.

Beginning Blends	Word Endings
sk	ub
pl	unk
str	ab
cr	ant
scr	ing

_____

- - - - - - - - - - - -

_____

- - - - - - - - - - - -

_____

- - - - - - - - - - - -

_____

- - - - - - - - - - - -

_____

- - - - - - - - - - - -

Find the Blend

SKILL: SPELLING WORDS WITH BEGINNING BLENDS

Say the word for each picture. Circle the blend that is missing from the word below it. Then write the blend on the line to complete the word.

____ ____ og	____ ____ ide	____ ____ ag
gr fr fl	sc sl sk	fl sl fr
____ ____ ug	____ ____ eep	____ ____ ap
gl pr pl	st fl sl	cr fr cl

Hidden S Blends

SKILL: IDENTIFYING BLENDS

Find the S-blend words in the picture. Read them and then circle them.

End Blends

SKILL: IDENTIFYING END BLENDS

Blends can be at the end of words—like gift, pact, camp, and felt.

Read each word, then circle the blend in the word.

gift	belt	lamp
hand	ant	cold
mask	bank	nest

End Blends Match-Up

SKILL: SPELLING WORDS WITH END BLENDS

Read the list of end blends. Then read the word beginnings. Draw a line to match each word beginning with an end blend to make a real word. Write each word on the line next to the picture that matches.

Word Beginnings	End Blends
po	ld
si	nt
go	sk
te	nd
ma	nk

Spelling End Blends

SKILL: SPELLING WORDS WITH END BLENDS

Spell each word by putting one letter in each of the boxes next to it.

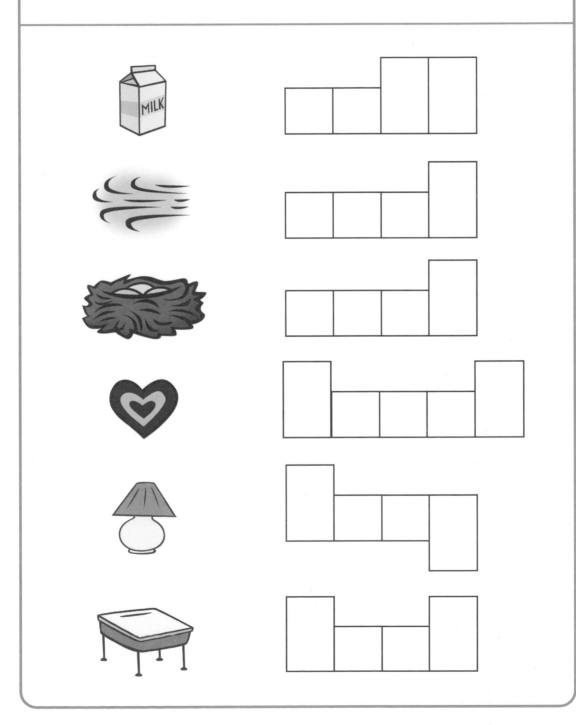

Blend Bank

SKILL: SPELLING WORDS WITH BLENDS

Yumi wants to spell these words, but she found out that sometimes blends are made up of three letters. Help Yumi borrow letters from the Blend Bank to fill in the missing three-letter blends. Then read the words you spelled.

scr   spl
spr   str

_____ _____ _____ a p e

_____ _____ _____ a s h

_____ _____ _____ a y

_____ _____ _____ a w

Balloon Blends

SKILL: READING WORDS WITH BLENDS

Read the word in each balloon. Color the balloons with two-letter blends blue. Color the balloons with three-letter blends green.

Circle the Blends

SKILL: IDENTIFYING BLENDS

Read each word below out loud. Circle the blend you see in the word. Then choose one word and write a sentence with it.

grin	plug	past
self	swim	cross
limp	trot	grab
sash	lunch	screw
crunch	skunk	brunch

Draw the Blend

SKILL: READING WORDS WITH BLENDS

Read each word. Then draw a picture of the word in the box.

toast	jump
star	smile
scream	dragon

Fill in the Missing Blends

SKILL: SPELLING WORDS WITH BLENDS

Fill in the blanks with the correct missing blends to make the word for each picture.

_____ own	_____ ag	_____ anet	_____ ess
_____ aw	co _____	mi _____	ba _____
_____ ay	_____ ane	inse _____	_____ are

Word Match

SKILL: SPELLING WORDS WITH BLENDS

Draw a line from each word beginning to a word ending to make a real word.

Write each word on the line next to the picture that matches.

plan   tist

den   olf

st   et

g   ump

Watch Me Read with Blends!

SKILL: READING WORDS WITH BLENDS

Read the words in the word bank. Then read the story. Complete each sentence by writing the correct word from the word bank on the line.

> smile, brush, clinic, spring, dentist

Eva is my _____.

I see her in the _____.

I see her at the _____.

Eva told me to _____.

She told me to _____

my teeth.

Skill 4: Digraphs

In this section, your child will learn to read and spell words with digraphs. A digraph is two letters that make one sound. These exercises will teach your child how to read words with the consonant digraphs /ng/, /wh/, /kn/, /ph/, /wh/, /wr/, and /ss/. Your child will also learn to read words with three-letter digraphs called trigraphs: /tch/, /nch/, /thr/, and /shr/.

Earlier your child learned about common vowel teams, also called vowel digraphs. In this section, they will learn more vowel teams: /ie/, /ue/, and /ui/. Some vowel digraphs are also called diphthongs. Diphthongs make a special vowel sound. This section will focus on /aw/, /au/, /ew/, /oo/, /oi/, /oy/, /ow/, and /ou/.

Here are three games you can play with your child to help them learn digraphs:

1. Help your child hear digraphs. Say, "King. Does *king* have the ng digraph?" Switch it up. Give a word and ask, "Does it have a digraph? If so, what letters make the digraph?"
2. Have your child notice digraphs when reading by playing Digraph Detectives. Say the letters, say the sound, and read the word.
3. Highlight digraphs in words. Have your child write or build words with digraphs. Ask your child to circle the digraph in the words.

Fishing for Digraphs

SKILL: IDENTIFYING WORDS WITH DIGRAPHS

Zack, Chet, Thad, and Cash went fishing. They put their fish all in one basket. Now they have to sort them. Can you help them?

Write the word with /ck/ in Zack's basket.
Write the word with /ch/ in Chet's basket.
Write the word with /th/ in Thad's basket.
Write the word with /sh/ in Cash's basket.

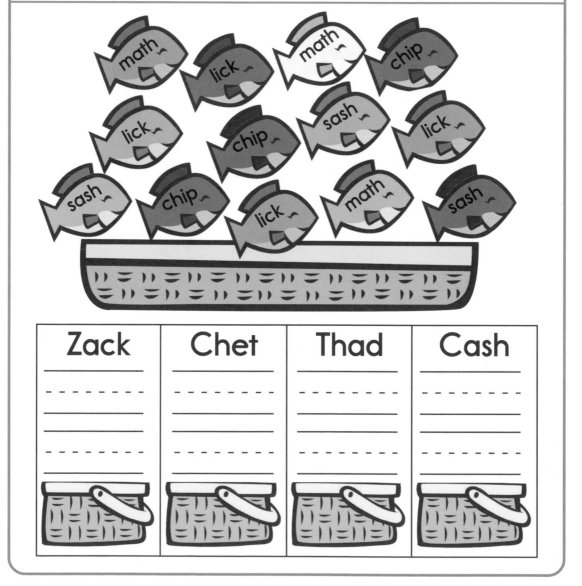

Zack	Chet	Thad	Cash

Color-by-Digraphs!

SKILL: IDENTIFYING WORDS WITH DIGRAPHS

Read the words in the scene.

Color the spaces with /ck/ words blue.
Color the spaces with /th/ words brown.
Color the spaces with /ch/ words green.
Color the spaces with /sh/ words orange.

the

thud

math

chop

chill

push

dock

chimp

chip

dash

shell

sick

pick

chin

chat

chomp

rich

with

moth

bath

A Maze of /Ch/

SKILL: READING WORDS WITH DIGRAPHS

Follow the words with /ch/, /tch/, and /nch/ through the maze to help the fly get to lunch.

125 More Learn to Read Activities

Listen for the Digraph

SKILL: IDENTIFYING DIGRAPHS

Say the word for each picture. Color the B box if the digraph is at the beginning of the word. Color the E box if the digraph is at the end of the word.

(sandwich)	B	**E**
(matchbox)	B	E
(fish)	B	E
(chair)	B	E
(bath)	B	E

Which Digraph?

SKILL: SPELLING WORDS WITH DIGRAPHS

Say the word for each picture. Then circle the correct digraph to spell the word.

__ __ __ eel	__ __ __ one	__ __ __ ist
wr kn ng	th ch ph	wr ss ck
si __ __ __	__ __ __ istle	dre __ __ __
ch ng th	th ck wh	ss sh ch

Word Chains

SKILL: SPELLING AND READING WORDS WITH DIGRAPHS

Read each clue. Follow the directions in the clue to write a new word.
Read the word you wrote. Use the word bank if you get stuck.

clutch, shrill, crunch, thrill, chunk, shrunk

	ill
Add /thr/ to ill.	
Change /thr/ to /shr/.	
Change /ill/ to /unk/.	
Change /shr/ to /ch/.	
Change /h/ to /r/ and /k/ to /ch/.	
Change /r/ to /l/ and /n/ to /t/.	

Draw the Digraph

SKILL: READING WORDS WITH DIGRAPHS

Read each word. Then draw a picture of the word in the box.

chat	itch
beach	ranch
bench	catch

Digraph Swim Team

SKILL: READING WORDS WITH DIGRAPHS

The vowel digraphs want to keep swimming—so let them swim!

Say the word for each picture around the pool. Then draw a line from the picture to the vowel digraph you hear in the word.

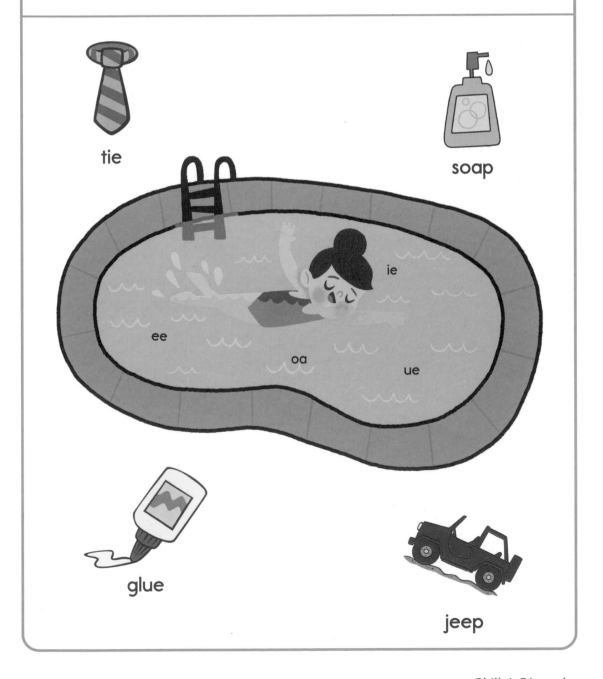

tie

soap

ie

ee

oa

ue

glue

jeep

Fill in the Vowel

SKILL: SPELLING WORDS WITH DIGRAPHS

Say the word for each picture. Fill in the missing vowel to spell the word.

Vowels: a e i o u

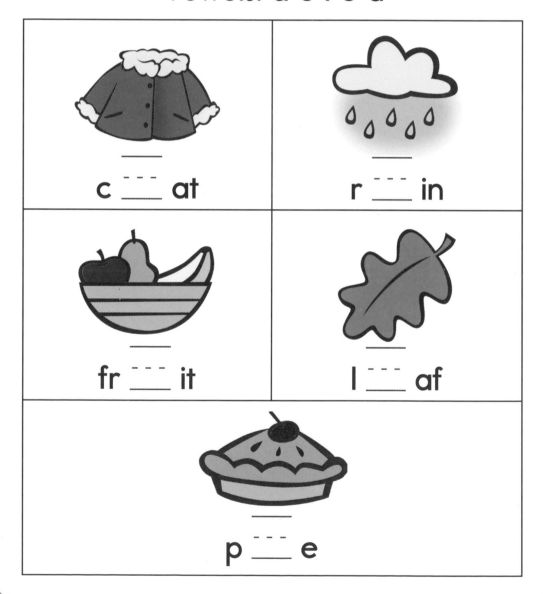

c _ _ _ at

r _ _ _ in

fr _ _ _ it

l _ _ _ af

p _ _ _ e

Darla's List

SKILL: READING WORDS WITH DIGRAPHS

Darla wants to learn these new sounds. Can you help? Say the word for each picture. Circle the vowel digraph in the word.

/aw/ /ew/ /oo/ /oi/ /oy/ /ow/ /ou/

 z o o

 h a w k

 c o i n

 b o y

 n e w s

 c o w

 m o u s e

Match the Digraph

SKILL: READING WORDS WITH DIGRAPHS

Say the word for each picture. Draw a line from the picture to the word that matches.

   spoon

   paw

   screw

   boil

   bow

Vowel Team Fix

SKILL: SPELLING WORDS WITH DIGRAPHS

These words are broken. Fix each word by circling the correct vowel digraph to complete it. Then write the vowel digraph on the line to fix the word.

p _ _ nt

ai   ea   oa

spr _ _ t

ou   ie   ai

b _ _ ns

ay   ea   ue

g _ _ l

ea   ie   oa

fr _ _ s

ai   ea   ie

_ _ l

ay   ow   ui

Catch That Digraph

SKILL: SPELLING WORDS WITH DIGRAPHS

Help Shae catch the letters for these words. Say the word for each picture. Draw a line to the missing vowel digraph.

h_____se   **ai**

d_____sy   **ou**

r_____d   **ue**

br_____m   **oo**

tiss_____   **ea**

Sentence Circles

SKILL: READING SENTENCES WITH DIGRAPHS

Read each sentence and circle the word that fits best.

The kids play / plan.

I have a sow / sock and it is

blue / block.

I have a bunch / lunch of cats.

Dan has the / three.

Sue Is Blue

SKILL: READING WORDS WITH DIGRAPHS

Read the words in the word bank. Then read the story.

Write the correct word from the word bank on each blank to complete the sentences.

food, candy, blue, plays, three

Sue is _____ .

Sue did not have much
_____
_____ .
_____

Sue _____ ball with Jamal.

Sue got _____ **3** and Jamal
got ten.

Mom felt bad and got Sue a gift.

Sue got _____ .

Sue is happy. ☺

Skill 5: Sight Words

A sight word is any word a child can read and spell automatically. Some of these words follow the rules, but others have irregular spellings. In this section, we will focus on learning the sequence of letters in these sight words: all, as, be, he, me, we, she, does, how, her, his, hers, do, to, of, or, word, were, what, they, said, when, one, and won.

The goal is for your child to be able to recognize these words instantly—or on sight. Use these tips to help your child memorize sight words:

1. Write sight words on index cards or pieces of paper. Hold up one word at a time and have your child read it. Make it fun and see how fast your child can read the stack of words.
2. Play Sight Word Detective! Post sight words around your house for your child to read each time they pass. Also have your child find sight words in books.
3. Help your child memorize the irregular spellings of sight words by underlining the tricky part of the letter(s) so your child learns the part of the word that they need to memorize (i.e., s<u>ai</u>d a<u>s</u> <u>of</u>).

Read Me!

SKILL: READING SIGHT WORDS

Touch the dot under each word while you read each sentence. Put a checkmark in the box at the end of each sentence when you finish reading it.

I am Jill. ☐

This is my school. ☐

This is Kim and Jim. ☐

I was in class with them. ☐

We are friends. ☐

Picture It!

SKILL: READING SIGHT WORDS

Read each sentence.

Picture the scene in your brain .

Draw a line to the picture the sentence is describing.

I was fast in the snow.

I am at bat.

This is spring.

I have to shop.

We have fun at the beach.

Citrus Sight Words

SKILL: READING SIGHT WORDS

Let's learn some new sight words!

Color the fruit pink if it has the word were.
Color the fruit green if it has the word what.
Color the fruit yellow if it has the word they.
Color the fruit orange if it has the word how.

Sweet Sentences

SKILL: READING SIGHT WORDS

Read the beginning of each sentence on the ice-cream scoop.

Draw a line to match the ice-cream scoop to its cone to make a complete sentence.

They were at

and a dog.

I have a cat

this for?

What is

home.

Sight Word Spy

SKILL: READING SIGHT WORDS

You know the word "we," so let's learn some of its rhyming friends: he, she, me, we, be.

Be a word spy and find these words in the picture below! Then follow these directions:

Circle the word we.
Underline the word _she_.
Double underline the word _he_.
Box the word me.
Make a squiggle under the word _be_.

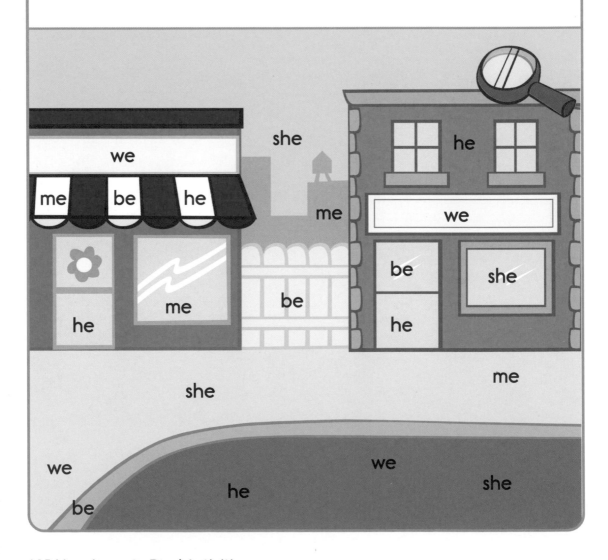

Question Clean Up

SKILL: READING SIGHT WORDS

Ren had a spill. Read each question. Draw a line to the picture that answers the question about Ren's spill.

What is on the sink?	rag mop
Is the spill big or small?	big small
What did Ren use to clean?	mop rag
Are there six flowers in the vase?	yes no

Sal's Sight Words

SKILL: READING SIGHT WORDS

Sal said he lost sight words when he fell. Help him put his sentences back together. Read each sentence. Fill in the sight word to complete the sentence.

Sal's Sight Words

her, when, said, all

_____

Sal said he fell _____ he got to school.

_____

Sal said when he fell, _____ the kids saw him.

_____

Sal _____ he fell when Kim made him trip.

_____

Kim said Sal did not trip on _____ backpack.

_____

Kim _____ her backpack is red.

Color the Bees

SKILL: READING SIGHT WORDS

The bees are buzzing with sight words that end in the /z/ sound. Color each bee following these rules:

Color the "is" bees blue.
Color the "his" bees green.
Color the "as" bees purple.
Color the "was" bees yellow.
Color the "hers" bees red.
Color the "does" bees orange.

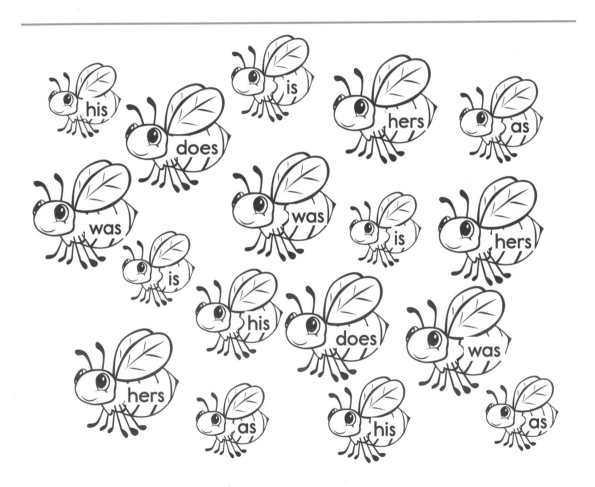

Rhyming Sight Words

SKILL: READING SIGHT WORDS

Read all the words in each row. Circle the two words that rhyme.

he have the she
for and or is
in you were her
by my we am
I me are we

Circle the Sight Word

SKILL: READING SIGHT WORDS

Read each sentence and circle the word that fits best.

What / They are the cats up to?

He sad / said to call mom.

She / His socks are green.

We were / does at the shop.

As / Is that her / he dog?

Finish My Picture

SKILL: READING SIGHT WORDS

Hana drew this picture! If you help her finish it, it will teach you a new sight word. Follow these directions to finish this picture.

Color my cat orange.

Color all my dogs brown.

Color my turtle green.

Color my fishbowl blue.

Color my parrot yellow.

What sight word did I teach you?

_____

- -

_____

Spin the Sight Word

SKILL: READING SIGHT WORDS

Which word will win? Use the tip of a pencil to hold the loop of a paper clip in the center of the circle. Flick the paperclip. Read the word that the paperclip lands on. Write the word on a line below. Repeat until you have a word on every line.

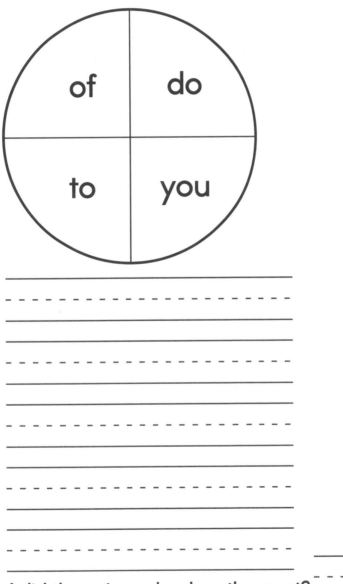

Which word did the spinner land on the most? _____

One or Won?

SKILL: READING SIGHT WORDS

These two sight words sound the same, but do not look the same.

Sound them out:

o   n e

w o   n

Write one or won on each line to make the sentences make sense.

Cam _____ the game.

_____ kid sat on the bench.

Ann _____ the prize.

The man has _____ cat.

Word Ladders

SKILL: READING SIGHT WORDS

Follow the **or** words to get to the end!

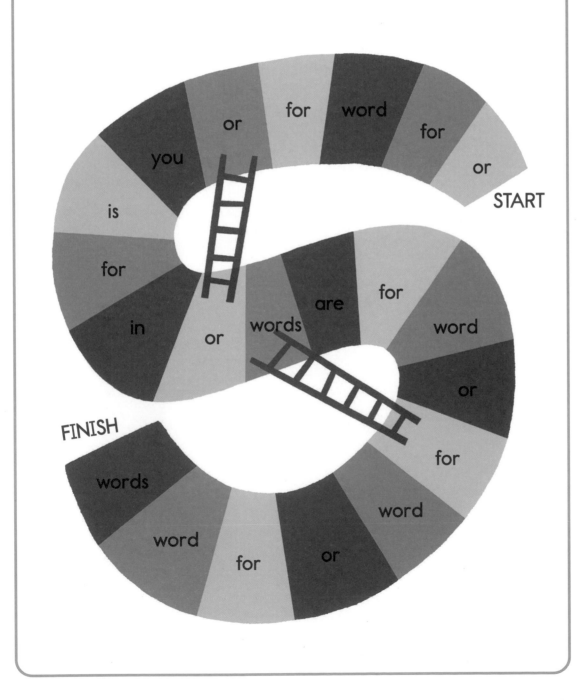

Words to Sentences

SKILL: READING SIGHT WORDS

Li has some jars of words. Help Li arrange the words in her jars to make sentences. Write each sentence on the line provided.

one
won We
prize

the dress
she
Does
have

Her to
mom
call said

What
her
is
name

Skill 6: Syllables

A syllable is a word part. Knowing how to divide words into syllables helps a child read multisyllabic words and gives them clues about the vowel sounds in a word. The goal is for children to mentally break up multisyllabic words as they read, so they can read them quickly and easily. Children start this process by learning to identify the syllables they hear in words. Then you can teach your child the rules of syllable division.

Help your child identify syllables in words with these tips:

1. Clap out the syllables in a word. Hold your hands far apart and make a big clap for each syllable. Have fun with it and clap out the syllables in people's names, places, and more.

2. Help your child learn syllable division by having them look at a word, circle the vowels in red, underline the consonants between the vowels in blue, identify the syllable division rule (VC/CV, V/CV, VC/V, or V/V), divide the word, and read it. Activities 84, 86, and 88 in this section will help make this clear.

3. When your child comes to a multisyllabic word in text, have them divide the word up by writing its syllables on separate whiteboards or sticky notes.

One-Syllable Maze

SKILL: READING ONE-SYLLABLE WORDS

Some words, like "cup," have one syllable. Follow the one-syllable words to help Spot get the ball back to Ken.

Clap It Out!

SKILL: COUNTING SYLLABLES

Clap the syllables in each word. First, hold your hands far apart.

Say the name of the picture.

Make a big clap for each syllable in the word.

Then write on the line how many syllables you counted in the word.

Say it! Clap it!	Write it!
fish	There is _____ syllable in fish.
crayon	There are _____ syllables in crayon.
muffin	There are _____ syllables in muffin.
owl	There is _____ syllable in owl.

ACTIVITY 82

Sweet Syllables

SKILL: COUNTING SYLLABLES

Read each word out loud. How many syllables does the word have? Color one candy next to the word for each syllable you hear.

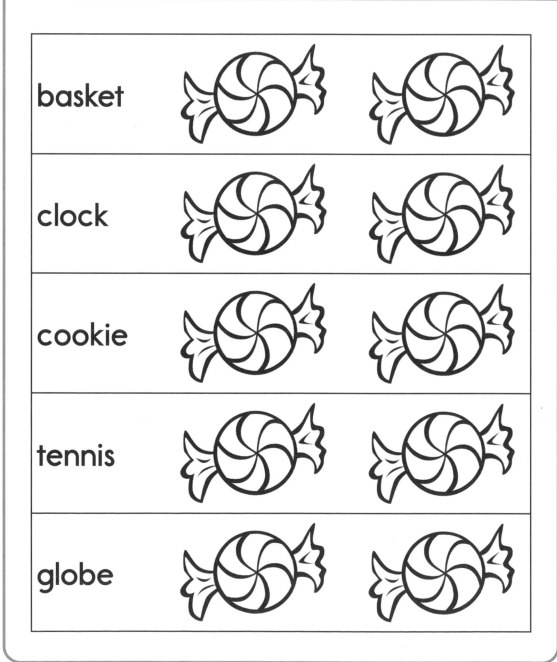

basket

clock

cookie

tennis

globe

88   125 More Learn to Read Activities

Sort the Syllables

SKILL: COUNTING SYLLABLES

Davi dropped his words. Help him sort them by syllables. Read each word. Figure out if it has one syllable or two. Write the word in the correct column.

candy   kitten   useful

duck   chill   shack

One-Syllable Words	Two-Syllable Words

Rae the Rabbit

SKILL: READING MULTISYLLABIC WORDS

VC/CV words have two syllables with a *vowel-consonant-consonant-vowel* pattern in the middle of the word. We divide these words into two syllables after the first consonant (i.e., rab/bit).

Help Rae the rabbit read these VC/CV words by following these steps.

Circle the vowels in red: r(a)b / b(i)t

Underline the consonants between the vowels in blue:
r(a)b / b(i)t

Touch the dot under each syllable to read the word.

den / tist

kit / ten

pic / nic

nap / kin

Read, Write, Match!

SKILL: READING MULTISYLLABIC WORDS

Touch the dot under each syllable to read each word.

Write the word on the line. Draw a line to the picture that matches the word.

rab / bit _____

pret / zel _____

cac / tus _____

par / rot _____

bas / ket _____

Tia the Tiger

SKILL: READING MULTISYLLABIC WORDS

V/CV words have two syllables with a *vowel-consonant-vowel* pattern in the middle of the word. We divide these words before the consonant if the first vowel has a long sound (i.e., ti/ger) or after the consonant if the vowel has a short sound (i.e., bal/ance).

Help Tia the tiger mark up the syllables to read these V/CV words by following these steps:

Circle the vowels in red. t(i)/ g(e)r

Underline the consonants between the vowels in blue. t(i)/ g(e)r

Touch the dot under each syllable to read the word.

bo / nus

lem / on

mu / sic

pi / lot

mod / el

fro / zen

Read, Write, Match!

SKILL: READING MULTISYLLABIC WORDS

Touch the dot under each syllable to read each word.

Write the word on the line. Draw a line to the picture that matches the word.

ti / ger _____

snea / ker _____

cam / el _____

liz / ard _____

ba / ker _____

Leo the Lion

SKILL: READING MULTISYLLABIC WORDS

V/V words have two syllables with a *vowel-vowel* pattern in the middle of the word. The vowels do *not* form a vowel team. We divide these words between the vowels (i.e., li/on).

Help Leo the lion mark up the syllables to read these V/V words by following these steps:

Circle the vowels in red. l(i) / (o) n

Touch the dot under each syllable to read the word.

di / al

fu / el

ru / in

li / ar

Read and Draw

SKILL: READING MULTISYLLABIC WORDS

Read each word. Then draw a picture of it in the box.

li on

gi ant

ti ger

rab bit

Which Word Type?

SKILL: READING MULTISYLLABIC WORDS

Are these words VC/CV, V/CV, or V/V two-syllable words? Let's find out!

Mark each word by following these steps:

Circle the vowels in red. ◯

Underline the consonants between the vowels in blue. ___

Touch the dot under each syllable to read the word.

Circle the word type.

picnic	VC/CV	V/CV	V/V
cabin	VC/CV	V/CV	V/V
poem	VC/CV	V/CV	V/V
music	VC/CV	V/CV	V/V
basket	VC/CV	V/CV	V/V

Syllable Spelling

SKILL: SPELLING MULTISYLLABIC WORDS

Spell each word by writing the missing letter on the blank.

sp ___ der

cac ___ us

pe ___ ny

l ___ on

pa ___ er

Syllable Coloring

SKILL: READING MULTISYLLABIC WORDS

Read each word.

If it is a VC/CV word, color it blue.

If it is a V/CV word, color it green.

If it is a V/V word, color it purple.

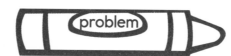

Syllable Match
SKILL: SPELLING MULTISYLLABIC WORDS

Draw a line between the first and second syllables to make five words.

soc   fin

ro   on

li   cer

muf   et

qui   bot

Syllable Sentences

SKILL: READING MULTISYLLABIC WORDS

Read each sentence and write in the word from the word bank that fits best.

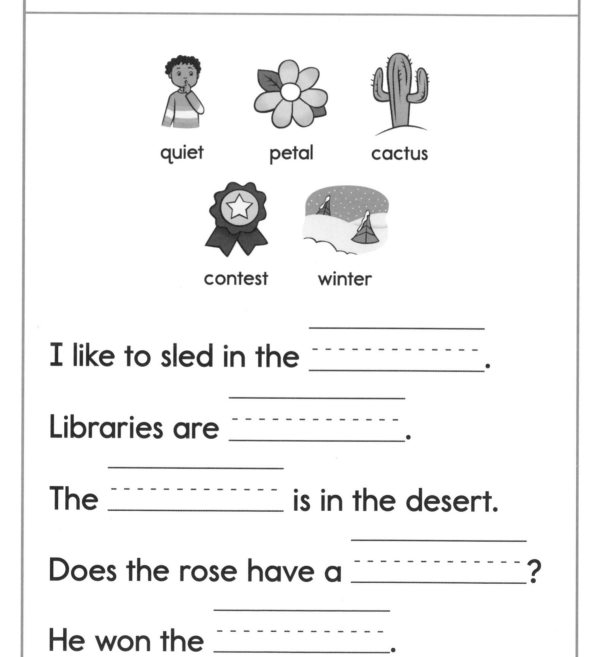

quiet   petal   cactus

contest   winter

I like to sled in the _____.

Libraries are _____.

The _____ is in the desert.

Does the rose have a _____?

He won the _____.

Skill 7: Compound Words

Compound words, like "pancake," are two simple words that have come together to form a new word with at least two syllables. It is important for children to see that when two simple words like /pan/ and /cake/ are connected, they create a new word with a new meaning. The goal of this section is for children to use their knowledge of closed syllables to read and spell compound words.

These tips can help you support your child in learning compound words:

1. Use pictures to introduce compound words. Show a picture of a pan and a picture of a cake. Then show a picture of a pancake.
2. Show your child how two words come together to make a new word. Write pan on one paper and cake on another. Put them together to show the word pancake.
3. Play compound word memory. Write the first syllable, or paste a picture, of a compound word on an index card and the second syllable on another. Do this for six words. Shuffle the cards, turn them upside down, and place them in even rows. Take turns flipping any two cards word-side-up. If the two cards make a compound word, you keep the match. Most matches wins.

Word Addition

SKILL: SPELLING COMPOUND WORDS

Complete each word addition problem to make a compound word. Write the new word on the line. Then read it!

  = _ _ _ _ _ _ _ _ _

rain + bow

  = _ _ _ _ _ _ _ _ _

paint + brush

  = _ _ _ _ _ _ _ _ _

cup + cake

  = _ _ _ _ _ _ _ _ _

door + bell

Barnyard Words

SKILL: READING COMPOUND WORDS

Circle the compound words in the barnyard.

treetop

skyline

barnyard

farm

horse

cow

horseshoe

chicken

sheep

pigpen

wheelbarrow

Compound Word Match

SKILL: READING COMPOUND WORDS

Say the name of each picture. Draw a line to match the picture to its word.

goldfish

cheeseburger

flashlight

mailbox

bathtub

Get to the Beehive

SKILL: READING COMPOUND WORDS

Follow the compound words to help the bee get back to the beehive.

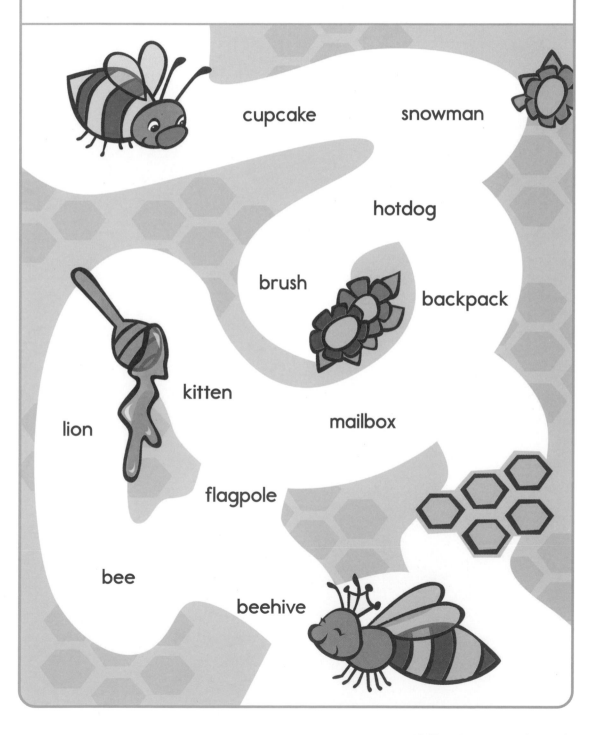

cupcake   snowman

hotdog

brush   backpack

kitten   mailbox

lion

flagpole

bee

beehive

Word Doctor

SKILL: READING COMPOUND WORDS

The doctor needs to know where to put the bandage. Read each word. Mark where the two words came together with a + sign. The first word has been done for you as an example.

bath+tub

baseball

rowboat

rainbow

drumstick

Compound Color

SKILL: SPELLING COMPOUND WORDS

Say the name of each picture in the left column. Color the two
pictures in its row that make the word for the picture.

	foot	oil	ball
	plane	cow	girl
	bug	bed	time
	rain	hand	coat
	lip	chair	stick

Make a Word

SKILL: SPELLING COMPOUND WORDS

Draw a line between the words and pictures in the left and right columns to make compound words.

air

fly

tea

bug

sand

The Ladybug's Sunflower

SKILL: READING COMPOUND WORDS

Read the words in this picture. Then color the ladybug and her sunflower.

Color the spaces with words that contain *mail* green.
Color the spaces with words that contain *shell* red.
Color the spaces with words that contain *fish* yellow.

How's It Spelled?

SKILL: SPELLING COMPOUND WORDS

Say the name of each picture. Circle the correct word spelling for the picture.

firefly   firfly   fireflie

seeshel   seashel   seashell

snowman   sowman   snoman

flapol   flagpole   flagpol

Draw That Compound Word!

SKILL: READING COMPOUND WORDS

Read each word, then draw a picture of it in the box provided.

rainbow	bathtub
hotdog	sailboat

Compound Sentence Circle

SKILL: READING COMPOUND WORDS

Circle the correct word to complete each sentence.

Mom had a bath in the

bathtub / sailboat.

Asad ate baseballs / pancakes.

Dara said to get her a

hamburger / barnyard at the shop.

The man said he got a

seashell / snowman on the beach.

Compound Word Snowpeople

SKILL: SPELLING COMPOUND WORDS

Finish each compound word snowman by writing in the missing word part.

Finish the Sentences

SKILL: READING COMPOUND WORDS

Read each sentence. Then write the compound word on the line that completes the sentence. A picture of the compound word is provided to help you.

He got his mail from the _____ .

Does she have her _____ lunch in her _____?

I play _____ .

She went to sleep at _____ .

The girl ate a _____ .

Spell the Compound Words

SKILL: SPELLING COMPOUND WORDS

Say the name of each picture. Fill in the missing letters to spell the word.

rainc ___ at

han ___ b ___ g

campf ___ re

___ ailb ___ x

b ___ sebal

r ___ in ___ ow

Finish the Story

SKILL: READING COMPOUND WORDS

Read the paragraph. Write a word from the word jar on each line to complete the story.

campfire

flashlight

bathtub   raincoat

bedtime

backpack

Cam and I went to camp. I put my clothes in my

_____ _____.

It got cold, so we made a _____.

I had a _____ to see at night. We went to

sleep at _____. There was rain the next day.

I put on my _____. I fell in the mud on the

way home. I got clean in the _____.

Skill 8: Prefix and Suffix/ Inflectional Endings

In this section, your child will learn about prefixes and suffixes. They will learn that a base word can stand alone with its own meaning. When a prefix (/un-/, /re-/, /pre-/, /mis-/) is added to the *beginning* of a base word, its meaning changes.

A suffix is added to the *end* of a base word. The suffixes your child will learn in this section (/-s/, /-es/, /-ing/, /-ed /, /-ful/, /-less/) are called inflectional endings. These change the number or tense of a base word.

Here are three tips to help your child learn prefixes and suffixes:

1. Help your child recognize base words. Have them underline the base word and circle the prefix and/or suffix in the word.
2. Give your child a base word to write in black crayon. Give them a prefix to add to the base word in green crayon. Suffixes can be written in blue crayon. Talk about how the meaning of the base word changed.
3. Teach your child a mnemonic device to remember the difference between a prefix and a suffix. The acronym P.S. can be used to help remember that a prefix is at the beginning of a word and a suffix is at the end.

Unlucky Lucy

SKILL: IDENTIFYING PREFIXES

Lucy's ice cream fell off her cone and onto the street. Lucy was unlucky!

The prefix /un-/ means "not." Mark each /un-/ word using the steps below:

Read the word.

Underline the base word (un<u>lucky</u>).

Circle the prefix (︵un︶lucky).

unload

unlock

unpack

unkind

unwell

Ready to Read and Reread

SKILL: READING WORDS WITH A PREFIX

Dustin reads all the time. He reads the same book over and over. He loves to reread his favorite books. Sometimes he prepays for his books before he picks them up from the store.

The prefix /re-/ means "again." The prefix /pre-/ means "before." Mark each word using the steps below:

Read the word.

Underline the base word (re<u>read</u>).

Circle the prefix (⟮re⟯read).

Circle the definition of the word.

reread	read again	read before	not read
prepay	not pay	pay before	pay again
repack	not pack	pack again	pack before
pretest	test before	not test	test again

Prefix Match

SKILL: READING WORDS WITH A PREFIX

Read each word. Draw a line to match the word with the correct definition.

> The prefix /un-/ means "not."
>
> The prefix /re-/ means "again."
>
> The prefix /pre-/ means "before."

unlock	fill again
refill	not clean
unclean	heat before
preheat	do again
redo	not lock

Don't Mis- the Prefix

SKILL: READING WORDS WITH PREFIXES

Carmen's dog took her socks. Carmen thought she misplaced her socks.

The prefix /mis-/ means "wrongly."

Read each sentence. Circle all of the words with the prefix /mis-/.

Then choose one sentence and draw it below.

Chad lost his watch. He had to tell his mom that he did misplace it.

Kala made a mistake in class. Her face got red.

He did misspell one word on his spelling test.

Beth had a red sock and a blue sock. She had a mismatch.

Prefix Fish

SKILL: READING WORDS WITH PREFIXES

Read the words on the fish. Then color the fish.

Color the fish part green if the word has the prefix /un-/.
Color the fish part blue if the word has the prefix /mis-/.
Color the fish part red if the word has the prefix /re-/.
Color the fish part yellow if the word has the prefix /pre-/.

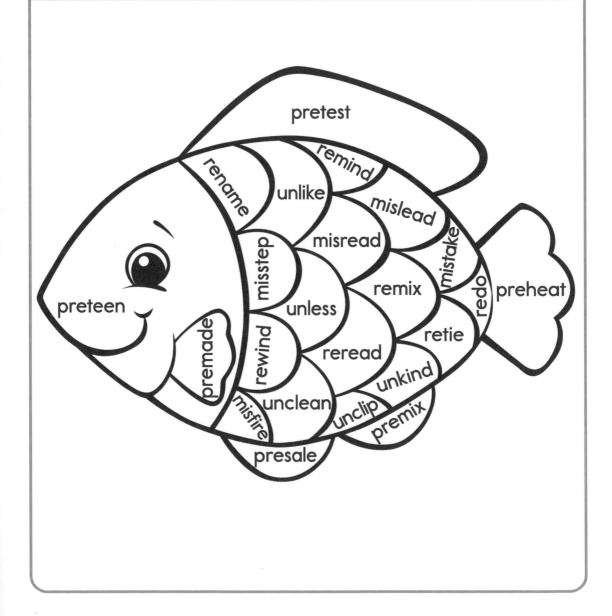

Stolen Prefixes

SKILL: SPELLING WORDS WITH PREFIXES

Someone stole the prefixes to words in the sentences below! Read each sentence. Write the stolen prefixes on the lines.

I made a mess so I had to _____ take my test.

The man was mean and _____ kind.

I _____ place my pack all the time and

need to look for it.

We can _____ pay so we can go in

before them.

Can I _____ wrap the gift?

un-   pre-

re-   mis-

The Prefix Prize

SKILL: READING WORDS WITH PREFIXES

Follow the words with prefixes to help the fox unlock the chest.

Match the Suffix

SKILL: SPELLING WORDS WITH SUFFIXES

The suffixes /-s/ and /-es/ help us name more than one person, place, or thing (make something plural).

Add the suffix /-es/ if the word ends in /s/, /sh/, /ch/, /x/, or /z/.

Add the suffix /-s/ if the word ends in any other letter.

Read each word. Match the word to the correct suffix to make it plural.

box		**s** **es**
peach		**s** **es**
coat		**s** **es**
dish		**s** **es**
sock		**s** **es**

Which Suffix?

SKILL: SPELLING WORDS WITH SUFFIXES

Read each word. Add the suffix /-s/ or /-es/ to the word
to make it plural.

Add suffix /-es/ if the word ends in /s/, /sh/, /ch/, /x/, or /z/.

Add the suffix /-s/ if the word ends in any other letter.

 dress + _____

 crayon + _____

 **sandwich +** _____

 flower + _____

 fox + _____

It's in the Past

SKILL: READING WORDS WITH SUFFIXES

Chad's dog got out of the house last night. He jumped on Chad's

trampoline. Now he is in a time-out.

The suffix /-ed/ gets added to a word to show that something happened in the past. Mark each /-ed/ word using the steps below:

Read the word.

Underline the base word (<u>jump</u>ed).

Circle the suffix (<u>jump</u>(ed)).

tossed

packed

asked

talked

yelled

Filling the Blanks

SKILL: READING WORDS WITH SUFFIXES

The suffix /-ing/ gets added to a word to show that something is happening right now.

Complete each sentence by writing an /-ing/ word from the word bank on the line.

drinking, going, flying, playing, working

The plane is _____ in the sky. ✈

Jace is _____ to school. 🏫

She was _____ with her dog. 🚶

He is _____ from the cup. 🧃

Maya is _____ on her homework. ✏

Useful or Useless?

SKILL: READING WORDS WITH SUFFIXES

The suffix /-ful/ means "full of." The suffix /-less/ means "without."

Read each word.

Draw a line from the word to the meaning of the word.

hopeful	without pain
helpless	full of help
useful	full of hope
painless	without use
helpful	full of use
useless	without help

Suffix Questions

SKILL: READING WORDS WITH SUFFIXES

Read each question. Draw a line to match the question to its answer.

What am I if I am
full of color?

playful

What is it called if my
laptop does not need
a wire?

cloudless

What is my dog if he
is full of play?

wireless

What am I if I am
full of tears?

colorful

What kind of day am
I without clouds?

tearful

The Suffix Circus

SKILL: READING WORDS WITH SUFFIXES

Read the words at the circus.

Circle the words that have a suffix.

seeing
tasteless
cats
redid
unhappy
jumped
tall
return
preplan
boxes
painful

What's Hidden?

SKILL: READING WORDS WITH PREFIXES AND SUFFIXES

Read and color the shapes in the box to reveal the hidden picture!

Color the words with a prefix blue.
Color the words with a suffix green.

Are you feeling extra smart? Circle each prefix or suffix with a black crayon.

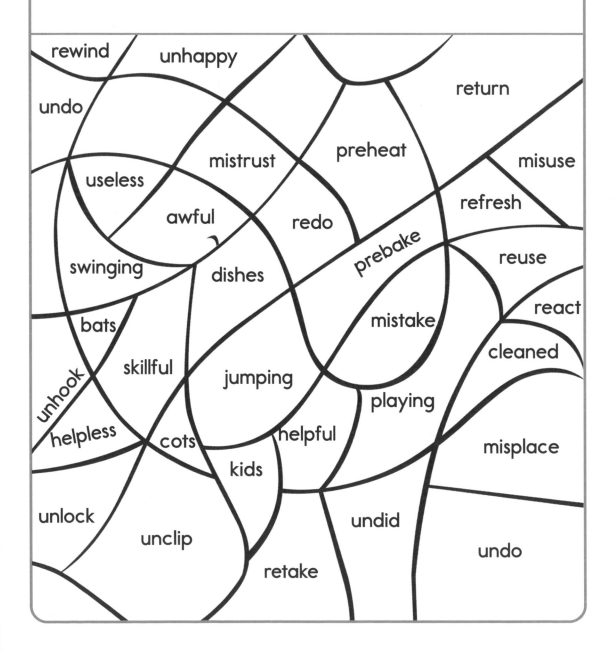

Prefix and Suffix Sentences

SKILL: READING WORDS WITH PREFIXES AND SUFFIXES

Read each sentence. Choose a word from the word bank to complete the sentence and write it on the line.

ACTIVITY
125

mistake, fishing, jumps, hooks, careful, playful, unhooks

Ava is _____ at the lake.
Her dog Sam came with her. Sam loves to play. He

is _____ .

Sam _____ in

the lake. Ava hopes it was not a

_____ to bring Sam

to the lake.

Ava _____

a fish. She has to be _____

with the hook. She

_____ the fish.

Ava drops the fish. Sam eats the fish!

Skill 8: Prefix and Suffix/Inflectional Endings   **133**

ANSWER KEY

SKILL 1: WORD SOUNDS

ACTIVITY 1
Let's Review A to M

*Keywords should be colored.

ACTIVITY 2
Let's Review N to Z

*Keywords should be colored.

ACTIVITY 3
Blend and Match

Lines should be drawn to the pictures in the following order:

box

mug

sit

pen

map

ACTIVITY 4
Blending and Circling

can

cub

bag

web

pig

ACTIVITY 5
Rhyme Time

The maze should be in the following order:

dog

hog

jog

log

fog

dog

ACTIVITY 6
Circle First

These letters should be circled in the boxes.

r-p-l

b-j-c

v-m-w

ACTIVITY 7
Circle Last

d-r-g

m-t-g

p-b-x

ACTIVITY 8
Beginning Match

c

b

j

s

l

ACTIVITY 9
Ending Match

p

sh

k

g

r

ACTIVITY 10
Find That Shopper

Kat: cat-mat

Sam: ram-ham-yam

Dan: fan-pan

Jack: pack-snack

*Sam

ACTIVITY 11
Color the Sounds

The following boxes should be colored:

violin-vegetables

bell-ball-bed

bed-sad-mad

lamp-mop

ACTIVITY 12
First Sounds

y-l-b

c-m-f

d-p-j

ACTIVITY 13
Last Sounds

x-b-t

n-g-d

n-p-m

ACTIVITY 14
Shopping for Sounds

l

b

l

t

Letters in your cart: l, b, l, t

ACTIVITY 15
Sentence Match

cat

bat

mop

sit

ACTIVITY 16
Spell It!

desk

mop

dog

mug

top

jam

ACTIVITY 17
Word Detective

cat

bat

bag

big

pig

ACTIVITY 18
Complete the Sentences

sad

hot

log

fill

ball-bat

ACTIVITY 19
Write a Story

bush-dog-rat-cat-dog-rat

SKILL 2: VOWEL (AND Y) SOUNDS

ACTIVITY 20
Vowel Sound Circle

i

o (for pot) or a (for pan)

a

u

e

ACTIVITY 21
Vowel Play

hat

hot

cot

cut

ACTIVITY 22
Colorful Caterpillar

Blue: bat, sash, lag, map, sat

Yellow: bell, net, pen

Green: pin, dip, fill, dig

Red: cot, hog, dot

Purple: fun, gut, cut, rush, bun

ACTIVITY 23
Baby Fly!

i-e-i

e-i-e

ACTIVITY 24
Vowel Shopping

Short /a/ Words

map

hat

Short /e/ Words

net

Short /i/ Words

mitt

Short /o/ Words

sock

Short /u/ Words

nut

ACTIVITY 25
Feather Fun

Blue: dam, mad, rag, back, ran, tap

Yellow: set, fed, pet, led, peg, fell

Green: big, lid, will, him, sip

Purple: pun

ACTIVITY 26
Vowel Roundup

lip-lip

bell-bell

nut-nut

a-e-i

a-a-u

ACTIVITY 27
Rhyme Time

shell

box

mop

bun

cat

tip

ACTIVITY 28
Run, Bud, Run!

Bud-cup-pun-bug-
nut-bun-sub-
but-run-tub-fun

ACTIVITY 29
The Train's Trip

pen

pig

cab

sun

ACTIVITY 30
Bossy E

can-cane

pin-pine

Rob-robe

tub-tube

ACTIVITY 31
Say the Vowel Name

cape-note-kite-cone

bike-cube-cake-mule

ACTIVITY 32
Vowel Teams

rain-A

boat-O

sheep-E

pie-I

ACTIVITY 33
Long and Short of It

Short /a/ Words

fat

Long /a/ Words

cave

bay

Short /e/ Words

pet

Long /e/ Words

meet

ACTIVITY 34
Sentence Circle

kite

home

cube

robe

SKILL 3: BLENDS

ACTIVITY 35
Star Blends

Color in: smell, skip, drop, clip, stop

ACTIVITY 36
Follow the Blends

flap-grab-stake-grip-blot-club-flag

ACTIVITY 37
Beginning Blends Match-Up

skunk
plant
string
crab
scrub

ACTIVITY 38
Find the Blend

fr-sl-fl
pl-sl-cl

ACTIVITY 39
Hidden S Blends

sniff
stop
slug
swap
smug
spill
snip
smoke
slip

ACTIVITY 40
End Blends

ft-lt-mp
nd-nt-ld
sk-nk-st

ACTIVITY 41
End Blends Match-Up

pond
sink
gold
tent
mask

ACTIVITY 42
Spelling End Blends

milk
wind
nest
heart
lamp
desk

ACTIVITY 43
Blend Bank

scrape
splash
spray
straw

ACTIVITY 44
Balloon Blends

Blue: star, trap, slide, clog, grub, skate, stop, sport, spit, play, swam, snap, plow
Green: split, spring, string, strap, spree, strong, scrap, scram, split, spray, splat, strip

ACTIVITY 45
Circle the Blends

gr-pl-st

lf-sw-cr

mp-tr-gr

sh-nch-scr

cr/nch-sk/nk-br/nch

*Sentences may vary.

ACTIVITY 46
Draw the Blend

*Pictures may vary.

ACTIVITY 47
Fill in the Missing Blends

cl-fl-pl-dr

str-ld-lk-nd

spr-cr-ct-squ

ACTIVITY 48
Word Match

planet

dentist

stump

golf

ACTIVITY 49
Watch Me Read with Blends!

dentist

spring

clinic

smile

brush

SKILL 4: DIGRAPHS
ACTIVITY 50
Fishing for Digraphs

Zack-lick

Chet-chip

Thad-math

Cash-sash

ACTIVITY 51
Color-by-Digraphs!

Blue: dock, sick, pick

Brown: the, thud, math, with, moth, bath

Green: chill, chop, chip, chimp, chin, chomp, rich, chat

Orange: push, dash, shell

ACTIVITY 52
A Maze of /Ch/

chip-chop-match-pinch-fetch-punch-ranch-watch-munch-finch-lunch

ACTIVITY 53
Listen for the Digraph

E

B

E

B

E

ACTIVITY 54
Which Digraph?

kn-ph-wr

ng-wh-ss

ACTIVITY 55
Word Chains

thrill

shrill

shrunk

chunk

crunch

clutch

ACTIVITY 56
Draw the Digraph

*Pictures may vary.

ACTIVITY 57
Digraph Swim Team

tie-ie

glue-ue

jeep-ee

soap-oa

ACTIVITY 58
Fill in the Vowel

o a

u e

i

ACTIVITY 59
Darla's List

oo

aw

oi

oy

ew

ow

ou

ACTIVITY 60
Match the Digraph

bow

paw

boil

spoon

screw

ACTIVITY 61
Vowel Team Fix

paint-ai

sprout-ou

beans-ea

goal-oa

fries-ie

owl-ow

ACTIVITY 62
Catch That Digraph

house-ou

daisy-ai

read-ea

broom-oo

tissue-ue

ACTIVITY 63
Sentence Circles

play

sock-blue

bunch

three

ACTIVITY 64
Sue Is Blue

blue

food

plays

three

candy

SKILL 5: SIGHT WORDS
ACTIVITY 65
Read Me!

*All boxes should be checked.

ACTIVITY 66
Picture It!

I was fast in the snow.
- snowboarding
I am at bat. - baseball and bat
This is spring. - spring
I have to shop. - shopping
We have fun at the
beach. - beach

ACTIVITY 67
Citrus Sight Words

Pink: were

Green: what

Yellow: they

Orange: how

ACTIVITY 68
Sweet Sentences

They were at - home.

I have a cat - and a dog.

What is - this for?

ACTIVITY 69
Sight Word Spy

ACTIVITY 70
Question Clean Up

rag

big

mop

yes

ACTIVITY 71
Sal's Sight Words

when

all

said

her

said

ACTIVITY 72
Color the Bees

ACTIVITY 73
Rhyming Sight Words

he-she

for-or

were-her

by-my

me-we

ACTIVITY 74
Circle the Sight Word

What

said

His

were

Is-her

ACTIVITY 75
Finish My Picture

What word did I teach you? - my

ACTIVITY 76
Spin the Sight Word

n/a

ACTIVITY 77
One or Won?

won

One

won

one

ACTIVITY 78
Word Ladders

or

for

word

for

or

or

words

for

word

or

for

word

words

ACTIVITY 79
Words to Sentences

We won one prize.

Does she have the dress?

Her mom said to call.

What is her name?

SKILL 6: SYLLABLES

ACTIVITY 80
One-Syllable Maze

Spot-dog-ball-

it-shut-when-

jump-kit-Ken

ACTIVITY 81
Clap It Out!

1 clap - one

2 claps - two

2 claps - two

1 clap - one

ACTIVITY 82
Sweet Syllables

2 candies

1 candy

2 candies

2 candies

1 candy

ACTIVITY 83
Sort the Syllables

one-syllable words - duck, chill, shack

two-syllable words - candy, useful, kitten

ACTIVITY 84
Rae the Rabbit

dⓔn / tⓘst
kⓘt / tⓔn
pⓘc / nⓘc
nⓐp / kⓘn

ACTIVITY 85
Read, Write, Match!

rabbit
pretzel
cactus
parrot
basket

ACTIVITY 86
Tia the Tiger

bⓞ / nⓤs
lⓔm / ⓞn
mⓤ / sⓘc
pⓘ / lⓞt
mⓞd / ⓔl
frⓞ / zⓔn

ACTIVITY 87
Read, Write, Match!

tiger
sneaker
camel
lizard
baker

ACTIVITY 88
Leo the Lion

dⓘ / ⓐl
fⓤ / ⓔl
rⓤ / ⓘn
lⓘ / ⓐr

ACTIVITY 89
Read and Draw

*Pictures may vary
(lion-giant-tiger-rabbit).

ACTIVITY 90
Which Word Type?

pⓘc nⓘc - VC/CV
cⓐbⓘn - V/CV
pⓞⓔm - V/V
mⓤsⓘc - V/CV
bⓐskⓔt - VC/CV

ACTIVITY 91
Syllable Spelling

i
t
n
i
p

ACTIVITY 92
Syllable Coloring

diet - V/V - purple
lizard - V/CV - green
muffin - VC/CV - blue
problem - VC/CV - blue
duet - V/V - purple

ACTIVITY 93
Syllable Match

soc-cer
ro-bot
li-on
muf-fin
qui-et

ACTIVITY 94
Syllable Sentences

winter
quiet
cactus
petal
contest

SKILL 7:
COMPOUND WORDS

ACTIVITY 95
Word Addition

rainbow
paintbrush
cupcake
doorbell

ACTIVITY 96
Barnyard Words

Circle the following: barnyard
pigpen
skyline
wheelbarrow
treetop
horseshoe

ACTIVITY 97
Compound Word Match

flashlight
bathtub
goldfish
cheeseburger
mailbox

ACTIVITY 98
Get to the Beehive

cupcake-snowman-hotdog-backpack-mailbox-flagpole-beehive

ACTIVITY 99
Word Doctor

base + ball
row + boat
rain + bow
drum + stick

ACTIVITY 100
Compound Color

Color in:
foot-ball
cow-girl
bed-time
rain-coat
lip-stick

ACTIVITY 101
Make a Word

dragon-fly
air-plane
bed-bug
tea-spoon
sand-box

ACTIVITY 102
The Ladybug's Sunflower

Green - mailman, mailbox
Red - seashell, shellfish
Yellow - jellyfish, shellfish, catfish, goldfish, starfish

ACTIVITY 103
How's It Spelled?

firefly - seashell
snowman - flagpole

ACTIVITY 104
Draw That Compound Word!

*Pictures may vary

ACTIVITY 105
Compound Sentence Circle

bathtub
pancakes
hamburger
seashell

ACTIVITY 106
Compound Word Snowpeople

dragon-fly
base-ball
paint-brush
back-pack

ACTIVITY 107
Finish the Sentences

He got his mail from
the - mailbox
Does she have her lunch in
her - backpack
I play - football
She went to sleep at - bedtime
The girl ate a - hotdog

ACTIVITY 108
Spell the Compound Words

raincoat - handbag
campfire - mailbox
baseball - rainbow

ACTIVITY 109
Finish the Story

backpack
campfire
flashlight
bedtime
raincoat
bathtub

SKILL 8: PREFIX AND SUFFIX/INFLECTIONAL ENDINGS

ACTIVITY 110
Unlucky Lucy

(un)load
(un)lock
(un)pack
(un)kind
(un)well

ACTIVITY 111
Ready to Read and Reread

(re) read - read again
(pr) epay - pay before
(re) pack - pack again
(pr) etest - test before

ACTIVITY 112
Prefix Match

(un) lock - not lock
(re) fill - fill again
(un) clean - not clean
(pre) heat - heat before
(re) do - do again

ACTIVITY 113
Don't Mis- the Prefix

*Pictures may vary.

ACTIVITY 114
Prefix Fish

Green: unlike, unless, unclean, unclip, unkind,
Blue: misstep, misfire, misread, mislead, mistake
Red: rename, rewind, remind, reread, remix, redo, retie
Yellow: preteen, premade, pre-sale, pretest, premix, preheat

ACTIVITY 115
Stolen Prefixes

re
un
mis
pre
un

ACTIVITY 116
The Prefix Prize

unfit-unbox-prefix-
reprint-undress-mistrust-
repay-remix-pretend-
misfit-unlock

ACTIVITY 117
Match the Suffix

box-es
peach-es
coat-s
dish-es
sock-s

ACTIVITY 118
Which Suffix?

es
s
es
s
es

ACTIVITY 119
It's in the Past

toss (ed)
pack (ed)
ask (ed)
talk (ed)
yell (ed)

ACTIVITY 120
Filling the Blanks

flying
going
playing
drinking
working

ACTIVITY 121
Useful or Useless?

hopeful - full of hope
helpless - without help
useful - full of use
painless - without pain
helpful - full of help
useless - without use

ACTIVITY 122
Suffix Questions

What am I if I am full of color?
- colorful
What is it called if my laptop does not need a wire? - wireless
What is my dog if he is full of play? - playful
What am I if I am full of tears?
- tearful
What kind of day am I without clouds? - cloudless

ACTIVITY 123
The Suffix Circus

Circles should be around:

seeing

cats

tasteless

jumped

painful

boxes

ACTIVITY 124
What's Hidden?

*Hidden picture is a whale.
Blue: unclip, react, unlock, retake, preheat, reuse, prebake, undid, misuse, return, refresh, mistrust, misplace, redo, undo, unhappy, rewind, unhook, mistake
Green: helpful, jumping, bats, dishes, playing, swinging, cleaned, skillful, awful, helpless, kids, cots, useless

ACTIVITY 125
Prefix and Suffix Sentences

fishing - playful

jumps - mistake

hooks - careful - unhooks

ABOUT THE AUTHOR

 **Rae Pritchett** is a curriculum author and teacher specializing in special education and reading. Rae is a passionate educator with more than 20 years of teaching experience.

Rae loves reading, writing, and researching best practices for teaching children to read. She shares this knowledge on her blog, *Miss Rae's Room* (MissRaesRoom.com). She also teaches education courses through The Learning Tree PDN (TLTPDN.com), an online teaching college Rae co-owns with her husband, who is also a teacher.

Rae holds a master's degree in education, a CAGS in Educational Leadership, and is a certified dyslexia practitioner. In her free time, she enjoys hiking, exploring, and spending time with her husband and their chihuahua.

Follow Rae on Instagram @MissRaesRoom